Moses Kainwo

The
Seven Deadly Sins
A Collection of Poems
By
Moses Kainwo

Moses Kainwo

The Seven Deadly Sins: A Collection of Poems
Moses Kainwo

Published By Parables
September, 2020

All Rights Reserved. No part of this book may be reproduced or utilized in any form or by any means, electronic or mechanical, including photocopying, recording, or by any information storage and retrieval system, without permission in writing from the author.

ISBN 978-1-951497-95-8
Printed in the United States of America

Readers should be aware that Internet Web sites offered as citations and/or sources for further information may have been changed or disappeared between the time this was written and the time it is read.

The Seven Deadly Sins
A Collection of Poems
By
Moses Kainwo

Moses Kainwo

Dedication

Agnes Ndoumbe Bangura
My sister
Your chicks were hatched
With different colours of feathers
To take from earth its colours
And give to heaven the same

Contents

1. Contents
2. Foreword
3. Wealth Without Work
4. This Goldvish Phone in Diamond Race
5. Stones
6. This Telephone
7. What Might Go Wrong?
8. Who is Wealthy
9. Let Me Tell It
10. Workplace Saga
11. Pleasure Without Conscience
12. A Letter to My Distant Lover
13. Give Pleasure to the Lord
14. Pleasure
15. In the Catacombs
16. Lady I Heard You
17. In the Beginning
18. Lot Away from Sodom and Gomorrah
19. Rain on Me
20. I Love You
21. Song of My Days
22. Letter from John Killer to James Prey
23. Homes
24. Knowledge without Character
25. This Bicycle
26. The Sickness of the Sick
27. Why play up to Smallness
28. Yearning for Darkness
29. The Saints
30. God is a Warrior of Sorts
31. How now Pastor how?
32. The King is Coming
33. Commerce without MoralityGod is Faithful Still

34. A Letter to Darwin
35. Sucking Above Chewing
36. My Husband the Businessman
37. Where is my Free-Gold
38. Dinah
39. Science without Humanity
40. What did he bring?
41. DNA
42. My DNA
43. Miss Queen Bee
44. The Eyeless God
45. Message from Onan
46. Poet in Residence
47. Religion without Sacrifice
48. The Slave Bible
49. Sacrificed with Tears
50. god is posh
51. God is Standing there
52. The Missing Shepherd
53. Join a Queue
54. The Table of Sacrifice
55. My Funeral
56. Holy Interventions
57. Politics without Principle
58. a strong dance
59. How are the Mighty Fallen?
60. A Letter to the Auditor General
61. I Want A Wall
62. The Writing on the Wall
63. The Princess of My Heart
64. Let Me Be Wrong

Moses Kainwo

FOREWORD

An experience in Poetry

I have been at two different book launches in the recent past. Both of them were collections of poems, one by a Cameroonian author and the other by several Caucasian Irish authors. At the former, I was just a guest; at the latter I was invited to introduce the book. Two things, among many, struck me most about the poetry of those two books. First, poets are story-tellers. They just use a different language style to do so. This realisation is nothing new, for every living being (human and non-human) tells a story if we care to see, hear and understand it. Not all stories, of course, are verbalised. Second, poets are as much in the stories they tell as the people and things whose stories they tell. Again, this is not a new idea. We can only assign words to experiences that we have had or recognise. This is the function of language: to name our experiences. In sociological terms, the context of the poet is reflected in their poetry.

Relevance and accessible language

Kainwo has written a collection of poems that express and explore the stories of the context he is steeped in and he does so more deeply and broadly than anything I have read elsewhere on this subject. As a poet, theologian, Bible student, Christian pastor, father, and an avid reader of books and the times he lives in, Kainwo takes us on a tour de force in this collection of Fifty-six poems exploring diverse angles of the seven deadly social ills in pleasantly surprising and readily accessible ways I have never come across anywhere before. My initial introduction to poetry gave me the impression that poetry is not for the ordinary mind. This cannot be said about Kainwo's poems. He often uses language that is readily accessible and yet profoundly challenges one to reflect seriously on the taken-for-granted.

The Seven Deadly Sins

The idea of the Seven Deadly Sins under which title this collection of poems is issued has its origins in Christian tradition. They are envy, gluttony, greed (avarice), lust, pride, sloth (excessive laziness), and anger (wrath). Each has supporting scriptural texts. This list is believed to have been first organised under themes and uttered in a sermon delivered in Westminster Abbey on March 20, 1925 by an Anglican clergyman by the name of Frederick Lewis Donaldson who called them the '7 Deadly Social Evils'. The origin of the idea may, however, go as far back as the Desert Fathers in the Third Century AD. Mahatma Gandhi, one of the most famous political and religious figures of recent memory, used these themes to great effect in his weekly newspaper Young India on October 22, 1925.

One or other of the seven deadly sins has formed the subject matter of nearly 300 books, among which are Pride and Prejudice by Jane Austin, Vanity Fair by William Makepeace Thackeray, The Grapes of Wrath by John Steinbeck, Lust for Life by Irving Stone, and Sloth by Gilbert Herandez. There are more modern fictions informed by one or other of these themes like the Devil I Know by Claire Kilroy on the theme of avarice and Your Fathers, Where Are They? And the Prophets, Do They Live Forever? by Dave Eggers.

The popularity of these sins and the themes which have emerged around them in literary works across time is an indication of their core relevance to humanity; and this latest addition of works exploring the themes underlines this. Following the example of Frederick Lewis Donaldson and Mahatma Gandhi, the author groups this collection of poems under seven themes: Wealth without Work, Pleasure without Conscience, Knowledge without Character, Commerce without Morality, Science without Humanity, Religion without Sacrifice, and Politics without Principle.

To isolate any poems in this collection would be unfair as all of them hold their own. But pieces such as What Might Go Wrong, Give Pleasure to the Lord, The Sickness of the Sick, Sucking Above Chewing, Miss Queen Bee, The Slave Bible, and a strong, strong dance resonated very much with me given the context of the realities of dishonesty, corruption and fake existence in all their guises in our world today. Stones, Pleasure, Yearning for Darkness, One day Someday, The Eyeless God, god is posh, and Let Me Be Wrong immediately grabbed me with the realisation of how, to their detriment, people often choose the counterfeit and forsake the real.

But if I was forced to choose my favourite poem, it is this: Who is Wealthy? It is one of the simplest poems in this collection and yet carries within it a very profound truth for me. Wealth is often defined almost exclusively in terms of material things people possess. This poem broadens that definition in ways that acknowledge the wealth of many our world chooses to describe as poor.

What I Love About This Collection of Poems
While this collection of poems opens a window through which the author invites us to take a look at life as lived in his context, it would be a mistake to understand that context exclusively as his country. As I read the poems I got the distinct impression that the author's concerns have global resonance. This is not surprising as human vices are not a monopoly of anyone society. Besides that, the author's experience of life spans far beyond that of his country of origin.

Second, about a third of this collection of Kainwo's poems scan social experience through the lens of scripture, thereby giving them spiritual immediacy in an age which would readily discard Scripture as too ancient to have any real use for modern society and its needs. The author of these poems shows otherwise.

Third, the author introduces each of the seven sections of his book with a relevant scriptural text – a helpful introduction especially to those who may not be so conversant with the scriptures from which the idea of the Seven Deadly Sins has its origins. In addition to this, there are several poems in this collection which the author basis on specific scriptural texts. By so doing the author reminds us that whatever many literary works have been inspired by themes he addresses, their true source – scripture – must be acknowledged.

Fourth, Kainwo brings a much welcome freshness to old ideas, making it difficult to lay the book down once you have begun reading it. You will encounter a variety of writing styles in this volume – a testament of the author's admirable grasp of the English language. You will find in this collection of poems one, two, three, four, five, six, seven, eight, nine and ten liner stanzas.

Finally, given the times we live in with visible street battles between supporters of the left and right of politics, the 'strong man' phenomenon in politics, fake news, migrant crisis, Black Lives Matter movement, the speedy blurring of lines between what is and is not acceptable behaviour and the eroding of values that once seemed sacrosanct, this is a timely publication reminding us about social ills that may undo our civilisation and possibly ourselves. Kainwo's poems challenge us to face ourselves, question our own values, attitudes and actions, and judge whether or not we are victims or perpetrators of one or other of the seven cardinal social sins. More often than not the author skilfully helped me come to the conclusion that I was both. I see a vision of thousands benefitting from this collection of poems.

Concluding Thoughts
A couple of thoughts kept coming to me as I read this collection of poems. Let me share them with you before I finish.

First, I kept thinking about a gardener who dreams of fresh, organic lettuce. He finds out there is a patch of ground at the back of his house that can carry a few good plants of lettuce. He gets his gardening tools, clears the ground, digs the soil, gets out anything that might impede growth, plants his lettuce seeds, waters them, takes out the weeds, and looks after them until his fresh lettuce leaves are ready for harvesting.
Alas, his dream of having fresh, organic lettuce leaves has materialized. He can relish his bite of lettuce that once existed only in his mind. He can even let others have some of his lettuce; and they can decide how good or otherwise it tastes.

The second thought that kept coming to me was about a pregnant woman who carries her baby for about nine full months. During that period of gestation, she goes through days and weeks of highs and lows – the joy of knowing she is carrying a potential new life within her, the morning sickness, the experience of physical and mood changes, abnormal cravings, constant feelings of movement in the tummy, labour pains, and, alas, birth.

Those two thoughts describe a writer's life. Dreaming, imagining, carrying, cultivating, taming, domesticating, nurturing, and growing ideas until they are born in print for others to see and hold in their hands.

The poems Kainwo has put in our hands are a product of a journey. All of them invite us to dream, imagine another life, place, experience. Like a gardener and pregnant woman, writers can tell you something about the origins of their finished

product, so to speak. But in truth, it is not that easy to discern the root cause of any desire, imagination, craving, and longing. We have to just make do with the reality of its presence. We have to be grateful for its varied sources even though we may not know them all. And we have to be aware of their power to take on a life of their own. Sociologists rightly say if you want to remain in control of an idea do not write it down or say it out; for as soon as you do any of that, your idea may grow legs of its own. As Byron Curtis puts it:
'Speech or book is snarky stuff – it doesn't like our laws.
Wall it in, and out it runs – like a brook through prison bars'
(Byron Curtis)

Poetry, perhaps more than any other kind of writing lends itself most to this possibility. So, congratulations to this gardener, mother, and father of dreams, imaginations and ideas that he has made possible for us to see and hold in our hands. Thank you for giving us the permission to give them legs of our own. May we allow them to echo across the rivers, forests, mountains and valleys of human experience and imagination as we all join you to give them voice in ways each of us know best.

by Sahr J. Yambasu, PhD
Circuit Superintendent
St Patrick's Methodist Church
Patrick Street
Waterford, Ireland

Wealth without Work

"For listen! Hear the cries of the field workers whom you have cheated of their pay. The cries of those who harvest your fields have reached the ears of the LORD of Heaven's Armies." James 5:4 (NLT)

"For even when we were with you, this we commanded you, that if any would not work, neither should he eat." 2 Thessalonians 3:10 (KJV)

This Goldvish Phone in Diamond Race
(To Kosonike Koso-Thomas)

This GoldVish phone in diamond race
Will feed your ears with diamond dust
The same way the cheapest phones must
With no veiled fee for a fair face

These teeth of yours in golden rush
Will fill your mouth with gold in smiles
But would not make your tummy bite
Any better than my white teeth crush

This wedding ring with sapphire stone
May give you lesser love than none
Though your face as shiny as the sun
Will face the emptiness alone

I reached for the highest fruit
Forgetting how heights were banned
By the holy books which damned
The first recipients of loot

Stones

Excuse me, when did stones become money?
When did stones replicate our bread and tea?

They leave stones up, yet dig for stones down:
They will dig for stones that will adorn crowns.

They will dig for stones they might never find,
Even when they shine like light in the night.

Searching for gravel inside other gravels,
An idea not exhausted by shovels;

Making men into bore hole animals:
To compete with rats and snakes as pals.

What about the stones under beds of chiefs,
Believed to answer to most awesome briefs?

Why leave quick stones for dead to erect grits
Why revere your never-to-emerge wits

Rachel hid her man's stony gods where she chose
And they were silent and never ever rose

This Telephone

This telephone does the job
Day and night day in day out
On the back of ignorance
In this jungle of a city

My telephone brought me it
I mean this house that is now mine
A few calls were enough for that
In this jungle of a city

This telephone gave them my names
And the whole world knows me so
Such fake names such fake titles
In this jungle of a city

This telephone gave me my car
And with it my short-lived spouse
So earned like nothing ever earned
In this jungle of a city

And this laptop will tell its tale
Of its first home and owner
Humble unassuming upright
In this jungle of a city

This object of a telephone
Deserves its praise and handsome raise
For buying me so much more
In this jungle of a city

From Jacob to other prophets
To Satan the father of lies
I could be massively misled
In this jungle of a city

What Might Go Wrong?

What might go wrong
If I could be rich with no scratches
And pay for things with no actual pay
What indeed might go wrong

What might go wrong
If I could own more than my kin
And get legal help to just bag that
What indeed might go wrong

What might go wrong
If I draw from my neighbour's well
And keep mine locked when theirs is dry
What indeed might go wrong

What might go wrong
If you can be in business with no being
Only crossing to those that would cross back to you
What indeed might go wrong

What might go wrong
If I vet another's wealth beyond vetting
And like Ahab win the game at night
What indeed might go wrong

What might go wrong
If the game of football is played at night
And the host wins in the dark
What indeed might go wrong

Who is Wealthy?

Rescued out of hot-burning fire,
By a friend;
She is wealthy.

Saved from drowning at mid sea,
By a friend;
He is wealthy.

Defended, when offended,
By a friend;
She is wealthy.

Rejected, but accepted
By a friend;
He is wealthy.

Hungry, but fed
By a friend;
She is wealthy.

Tormented, but cemented
By a friend;
He is wealthy.

Defeated, but uplifted
By a friend;
She is wealthy.

In darkness, but given light
By a friend;
He is wealthy.

Let Me Tell It

Please please please please allow me to tell it
My story of genii that brought me wealth
They taught me to convert figures in books
And one multiplied itself to become four
Or sometimes one simply became one hundred
So am I not superfine

Please please please please allow me to tell it
How I got a job with a drug magnet
How like Cinderella's godmother
They showed him me among all the poor
Of this land from north to south east to west
So am I not superfine

Please please please please allow me to tell it
How other genii taught me to break locks
The hardest of locks or take the door whole
Making an easy gateway for transporting
Things shiny things from other homes to mine
So am I not superfine

Please please please please allow me to tell it
How I was trusted with stuff for innocence
Before they are old enough to take over
And how my genii taught me to make them mine
With a second stroke of my fountain pen
So am I not superfine

Please please please please allow me to tell it
How as Pastor I raised godly families
To become my Jacob's ladder to God
With their faithful giving as I taught
Day after day and Sunday after Sunday
So am I not superfine

Workplace Saga

management - filed   extra-management — filed
harassment - filed   saga - filed
lies - on the ground   lies - in the air
lies - untenured   first degree bigotry - well fed
first degree lust - well fed with underpay

business with structured setups
and so we laboured to do - with obligation to do
and to silently undo - with a silence to signatures
and now we are full
at thirty i am full
at forty i am full
at fifty i am so full
god help us

what happens at lunch time is anyone's guess
property borrowing with promise of returning forever
wife borrowing with promise of returning forever
husband borrowing with promise of returning forever
salaries nailed except...
promotions nailed except...
benefits nailed except...
is there a security camera
installed by whom

yet more enemies of progress
sicknesses
sackings
ageing
so take it so at fifty
if nothing private is hatched

Pleasure without Conscience

"For we ourselves also were sometimes foolish, disobedient, deceived, serving diverse lusts and pleasures, living in malice and envy, hateful and hating one another." Titus 3:3 (KJV)

A Letter to My Distant Lover

Honey,
we don't need to buy the panic
that the world has put on auction.

When you and I stand in any square,
we will be enveloped by true love,
love delivered by the esplanade of time.

Let the volcano erupt,
but don't allow it to throw you up,
into its own creation,
robed with Mrs Lot's gown.

Coming to think of it,
what can you do to change,
the years that nature pumped,
into our love life.

Oh, you, my long-lost crush;
I long for the magic,
that will lift me from here,
and land me at your feet.

Give Pleasure to the LORD
(Based on Isaiah 1: 10 – 20)

Come to me and give me pleasure
If you can erase murder from your mind
If you can print life boldly on your mind
You are justified to be where I am
So come to me and be my daughter or son

Come to me and give me pleasure
And be a donkey from now on
As you very well know
The donkey knows the secret to longevity
So come to me and be my daughter or son

Come to me and give me pleasure
Be a chimp and talk to me in sign language
When you are ashamed to face me
I will hear you from heaven my fireside place
So come to me and be my daughter or son

Come to me and give me pleasure
Watch your games if you must
But don't be the lazy mammal that lies all day
Enjoying doing nothing away from my pleasure
So come to me and be my daughter or son

Come to me and give me pleasure
Be the tamarin monkey that breaks its bread for family
And every family member is happy
I will be there to share your family-style meal
So come to me and be my daughter or son

Come to me and give me pleasure
Be a robin or songbird or nightingale
And like them let your tunes come from the heart
And I will hear you from your choir stall
So come and be my daughter or son

Come to me and give me pleasure
Be the Atlantic bottlenose dolphin
And work to promote family life
I will join you in such families
So come to me and be my daughter or son

Come to me and give me pleasure
Be not the howler monkey that doesn't believe in silence
Remember that the noise you make can kill
The healing I have given to my people
So come to me and be my daughter or son

Come to me and give me pleasure
Be a panda and observe good table etiquette
I love to eat with those who eat with discipline
They are neither greedy nor gluttonous
So come to me and be my daughter or son

Come to me and give me pleasure
Be a purple finch my daughter
The purple finch goes all out to make her house a home
Do the same for the sake of my pleasure
Then come to me and be my daughter or son

Come to me and give me pleasure
Be not the wild elk with its brutal strength for sex
But be a peacock with its seductive display of love
And even be monogamous like the beaver
Then come to me and be my daughter or son

Pleasure

I lay me down in the evening sun to bathe
On this beach that waited here before my mother was born
On this beach where people come and go
The gentle and the not-so-gentle come and go
Guests to this nation had lain themselves here like me
Indeed the setting sun has so much pleasure in it
Just as does the rising sun
So that dusk and dawn speak the same language
And at all times people are praying in the sun
This sun that was here before my mother's mother was born
Not only that but they will share stories as well
Stories before my great grandfather was born
They will open their eyes to watch the setting sun
Yes the sun is always setting since before my great great great grand parents
They in their hearts say farewell to the sun
Before it falls into the sea just like yesterday

In the Catacombs
(based on Luke 15: 11 - 32)

Sex paraded with big words slapping
And once in the dark
A father went to bed with his daughter
The daughter knew him but he did not
She remained silent and took the money
Before the telling
Before giving him the news
Before he promised to resign from the catacombs
Before he resigned from the catacombs
After the fact...

She stayed there in the Central Catacomb
Snatching the purses of all her guests in the dark
Never finishing the act with them
"Oh your time is up in the sky
I have another waiting on the ground
Get up lazy Jack get up
And engage a lazy snake looking for an egg to hatch
In the darkest part of the catacomb
In the darkest part of hell
After the fact..."

And the words big words to deafen the ears
Words of abuse not found in the marketplace
But he swallowed all for fear of not getting the asset
And returning home dry
With God and him knowing the case of their pants
HIV galore
Ebola galore
Food shortage galore
School fees shortage galore After the fact...
I must go now to my father and tell
He needs to meet his grown-up daughter
This time in the light of day

Away from the famous catacomb
The place of rebirth for generations before
And generations to come
I must ascend and give him this pregnancy
The fruit of his labour in the dark
Of the Central Catacomb
After the fact...

Lady I heard you

Lady I heard you
When you said
With very red lips
And posted eyelashes
On high heeled towers
Help me with my baby's medicine
So I ask again
Lady what would you have

I heard your workmate too
When she said
Help me get an AC at home
White teeth quoted yet punctuated by gold
With short skirt to sweep the air
So I ask myself
What is the job here
Lady what would you have

Lady I heard you
Only when you smiled by the quest
Believe me I heard you
Twisting your tongue
When you meant the opposite of something
Thinking my necktie and jacket
Smell of millions somewhere
Not called a bank

Lady I heard you
But did you hear me
When I smiled and giggled and spat
Before I said consider it done
And said I wish I could speak a poem
That would address your redress
And make you hear when I say
Lady I heard you

In the Beginning

In the beginning God created
Little things and big things
Little people and big people
Little trees and big trees
And created and created and created
Until he created the genesis of rest

In the end God ended
Big ways and small ways
Big skies and small skies
Big worlds and small worlds
Big fires and small fires
Until he revealed the chaos he hated creating

Somewhere in between the creatures created
Big worlds and small worlds
Big people and small people
Noisy stuff and quiet stuff
Big Gods and small gods
Until he created the demons

Again somewhere in between
The stars emerged from their dark corners
To salute the sun above the blue skies
And give Noah a rainbow
More magnificent than Cupid's bow and arrow
So that the earth laughed to receive the news

In the beginning there was no motor car
But the prophet of God went where God sent them
And got the required result
Rain fell where drought had threatened
The dead were raised in the power of the greatest Power
Yet it was only the beginning of the jet age

Lot Away From Sodom and Gomorrah

Swing low on Sodom
Or swing high on Gomorrah
It's a matter of where you stand
For manhood on manhood
Or womanhood on womanhood
But what does history say

Swing low very very low
Like snakes lying straight in the grass
Down there in Sodom and Gomorrah
True grandpa you have a price from heaven
For defending angels
But what does history say

Swing high very very high
Like monkeys among the forest trees
Up there in the mountain above Zoar
True grandpa Abraham prayed for you
But did you pray for yourself
And what does history say

Swing now from hotspot to hot spot
And ask the Moabites and Ammonites
Their part in the history of hatred on their heads
But tell the older daughter of her great granddaughter
Who escaped to Bethlehem
And what does history say

Rain On Me

Rain rain stay awake
Come today
Come tomorrow
Come on the morrow after

Lord Jesus
If you rain justice on me
I will not yearn for justice
If you rain religion on me
My soul will not do sacrifice
If you rain power on me
I will not conjure power
If you rain pleasure on me
I will not pursue pleasure

Drug me Lord Jesus
Drug me with your good news
So I can shout alleluia
When I face fretful faces
Oh rain on me and drug me
Drug me with your philosophy
So I can banish hungered philosophies
From my soul
Oh drug me with your love
Love that can interpret love to divided humans
Rain master Jesus rain
And flood the earth where I stand and sit and lie
With unmatchable truth
That will dispel sorrow and misery
And shower me with boldness
And the gift of silence even when bold
Rain on me

I Love You

The lightning from your eyes has pierced my soul
And nailed me to your cross
Your way of defining love towards me
And when my silly blood was wasted on the hill of answers
You poured your blood into my soul
And once again I came alive

When you brought your refill of blood into my soul
I had no doubt that you really loved me
So be not troubled when I touch you
It is because I really must touch love
Be not alarmed when I go for your lips
It is because I want to taste of true love

Everywhere I turned I heard the words I love you
And I said to myself this world is crazy
I even heard one bird say to another I love you
And the other spontaneously burst into a new song
That they both sang as if they had rehearsed the same
Allow me to whisper these same words into your ears
I love you

You carefully buried me in your heart
I now know it was deliberate that you struck me so
With lightning from those piercing eyes of yours
No one ever hit me with lightning like you do
No one ever hid me in their heart like you do
I have no doubt you have the power to possess

SONG OF MY DAYS

The song only came to me
A moment ago, and pulled
The string on days long ago;
And I promptly sang for her.
Oh how she loved it! She did.
My daughter really loved it.

I sang it as from those days—
A smart boy in uniform,
As if on that band, but no.
I sang lustily body,
But forgot the dance to it;
Though we danced so well to it.
The song started with "one child"
And the story of the rod
Giving way to the sung song,
Crept into her head there and then.

In that song,
The father stood in wonderment
Of a talent on the spot;
And my daughter said, Please dad,
Kindly give it to my mum,
And mummy will pass it on:
And I too will pass it on.
That song should never ever die:
It should pour from lips of old,
It should pour from lips today.
We do not need the drum beat,
We do not need the guitar."

I sang lustily body.
The guitar string on my throat
Was revamped from its twisted base;
No, it was not a rod.

No, it was not a pen either.
No, it was not a sword,
But it brought back a rod—
On my back on matty beds,
On my feet on stony ground,
On my crown of lessons,
Unequal to the flagellum;
Pilate's flagellum of blood:
And the tears dropped upon my chin,
And then my trembling lips,
Enheh—and then my chest,
But she said, "Please sing for me!
The song of your days,
Is indeed the song of my days.

I should sing it in the rain,
To wet my chin and chest.
Daddy, sing like you never sang—
The song of your days!
 Daddy, sing like you never sang—
The song of my days!
And so truly wet my chin,
And so truly wet my chest,
With the rain from inside,
As with song from your days.

Letter from John Killer to James Prey

Dear James
You shocked me so like never before
When you took my photos away
Plus your well-built mountains
Plus your smiles of deceit
Leaving me in the cold behind them all

Have you got a new killer
In the forest of doubts where you keep curling
In your lonely world from the world
Because they guessed what you and I did
Behind closed doors together
Before you took my photos away

Oh James
You used to love being hunted
Have you suddenly become the killer
Of lions or elephants or the serpent
Just let me know how you changed
Your skirt for a pair of trousers

HOMES

This is the mansion which I share with you:
X feet by Y feet by Z feet.

Look at that glass and say whose face you see:
The words take the shape of a soul,
As they hang there
Before my books.

Nothing less than an angel is that poem,
Nothing less that paradise for two is this room
Welcome home madam,
Queen the first of Kingdom Busy.

But you must go
Overseas
And devour bills
You may hit the bills
You may spit the meals
But the home pride
Bears sour fruit

Shambles under chandeliers,
The heavenly glows
Over there.

Where lives are curiously juxtaposed in perjury;
Marriage for convenience,
Marriage in series,
Marriage for strife,
Marriage for the dollar,
Marriage for the altar,
Marriage for the father,
The defaulter's game,
Ripens with the lawyer's gain.
There's home everywhere.

The homegivers rest on their oars,
The homeseekers meander the path
Like tired sheep for bed
The women name the world,
For the children.

Knowledge without Character

"Discretion is a life-giving fountain to those who possess it, but discipline is wasted on fools." Proverbs 16:22 (NLT)

This Bicycle

This bicycle is my best friend
Taking me where I want to ride
To gallop like a horse on a dusty road

Once gave me a story when it rode over a stone
And I nearly fell off her back
In the middle of the night

One day when I was far away from home
One tyre went flat and I could go no more
And yet I knew she had no temper

I had thought her the most faithful friend
Never disappointing in the middle of hope
That I could never be late because of its hunger

Imagine Satan who speaks the greatest speeches
Yet leads our first great grandparents to fall
What a fall there was always to be repeated

Not only does my bicycle make me fall sometimes
Nowhere near the ass that took the Master there
Wish I could have that one in place of her

Did I have a right to be proud of her
When we sometimes rode in peace
Yet sometimes rode in total mistrust

Yet I am so used to this bicycle
And even when I doubt I will always go for her
Because each time I fall I can rise again

The Sickness of the Sick

He told them he was sick
Whatever that word meant
He stayed away from work
But not away from food

He took a piece of paper
And wrote the word he loved
The teacher peeped and saw it
And granted him his sick leave

He knew what there was to do
But just couldn't do it
Yet would do the opposite
To give himself a field day

Coming to think of it
He really was sick in the head
For who in their right mind
Would ever forge their health downwards

Who would ever fly with lies
And say you are their true friend
When they don't know their own package
In your sick pouch

I am not strong but you can't be my pillar
Nor my pillow on a gallopy night
Because you will make me more sick
By the bundle of lies you will put on my head

You could very well be Amnon
Because you have seen Tamar
So go on and be ill from morning to night
Only remember that Absalom will never be sick

Why play up to Smallness

My friend you are afraid of nothing
When you pretend to be small

Even though you are great
Even though you are great

See how tall you are
See how wisdom-infested you are
Even though you live with fools
Even though you live with fools

Others pretend to be great but not you
Why be small yet keep standing on the peak
Even daring to sleep in the small
Even daring to sleep in the small

You have fathered and mothered greats
And by them the world sees you
Yet you tell them you are small
Yet you tell them you are small

Yearning for Darkness

We both did lie on the beach
And baked in the sun
Thinking we would be darker
Like the fire-baked brick

I have seen bleaching creams
That work like knife on pig skin
Under boiling water to be
What one was not meant to be

Maybe we will need new creams
For making dark or fire-baked stuff
Bricks that will last in the house
So they will stand beyond a lifetime

The Saints

Wingless creatures likewise created
Chose to shake the dirt off holiness
With likewise abilities gifted
The Creator called them as he did us
They heard the call and heeded it so

The men walked among finely-clad women
The women spoke to men six feet tall
Of course they fell like we daily do
But their hearts kept bouncing toward one goal
The "Well done" from the King up there

Each "Amen" from their trembling lips
Launched another "Thank You" to Christ
Each "Thank You" another lowly bend
Which the Lord in love embraced
See there a queue for my own loose lips

God is a Warrior of Sorts
(based on 1 Samuel 28: 4 - 25)

God is a warrior of sorts
On the plains of Philistia
In the valley of Baraka
Dealing deadly blows on them

God is a warrior of sorts
He will test you with your shadows
When the moon is parading
With great tunes from the blues

God is a warrior of sorts
Warring with Saul in his head
Warring with Moses in his eyes
Until a meaning drops for the world

How now Pastor how?

Do you remember?
You vowed to serve the master:
At the cost of dungeons,
At the cost of lions,
At the cost of lies against you,
And yet a little fly scared you
Almost to death. Almost!

Do you remember?
You claimed to be happiest
When serving in the least role;
But when the post was emptied
You nearly killed your best friend,
The most immediate threat
To the advantages of the package.

The King is Coming

The King has come
He keeps coming
Like two thousand years ago he came
Even last year he came
And the world was in a flashier tone than the year before
Even unlike two thousand years ago
    Flashy shops and shopping
    Flashy spouses well spiced on the moon
    Flashy cars bought with flashy cash
    Flashy children whose parents are haters of the manger
    Flashy garments that Mary never grabbed
Some will visit the sky beyond the moon
With jamba[1] and ɔmɔle[2] in the head
And dump the very things they just acquired
    The flashy shopping done over counters of flashy shops
    Flashy spouses that walked on the moon
    Flashy cars bought with flashy cash
    Flashy children uncared for by flashy parents
    Flashy garments for flashy eyes on the King's first visit

Hey wait a minute
There is another coming
Not to be fouled by any king or president
When the President of the universe lands
With a bang and answered by shouts from below
That should land us in heaven or hell
This time it is going to be an adult King
With precision in his voice
More than any judge you know
The King's coming brother
The King's coming sister

---

[1] *Marijuana*
[2] *Locally brewed alcohol*

It would matter little if you voted for his coming
Because even the gates of hell
Had better vote for him
He is coming whether we are ready to receive him or not
The King's coming
He will come and we are sure to see him
Kojuma koju[3]—Lonta[4]

---

[3] Face to face
[4] You are warned

Commerce without Morality

"So he invited each person who owed money to his employer to come and discuss the situation. He asked the first one, 'How much do you owe him?' The man replied, 'I owe him 100 measures of olive oil.' So the manager told him, 'Take the bill and quickly change it to 50 measures.' "   Luke 16: 5 - 6 (NLT)

God is Faithful Still

Sucked
Spat upon
Muddied
But God is faithful still

Paraded
Kicked
Beaten
But God is faithful still

Named
Abused
Abandoned
But God is faithful still

Denied
Rejected
Dumped
But God is faithful still

Gossiped
Maligned
Accused
But God is faithful still

Hanged
Hanged
Hanged
But God is faithful still

Loved
Loved
Loved
Yes God is faithful still

Letter to Darwin

Everything he touched
                Became gold
And there was salute to an amoeba
Whom they presented with gold
                          Plain gold
            In the arena of animals
      Suddenly
             The invisible became visible
And the Queen
                        Was Queen
      From the time she sat on the floor to crawl
For a piece of bread
            Thereby chewing the rug
                  Both when she was alone
    And when she was with them
Before the electric light was switched on
And Darwin said
                  In the hearing of everyone
That is a chimp that will rise to wear the gold
                              Mark it

One day Someday

One day someday
In a meeting
Of classes
You will see how abundance often greets the little
With scruple
Redundant
And mean
With gusto
In tongues
Well guessed
On the hill
With stripes

Sucking Above Chewing

If I take my other hand
To write my name
I would be translated into a child
That would suck its finger
And yet say no to food
With sucking preferred
Above chewing and licking

If I take my other leg
To kick a ball
I would be called amateur footballer
That would score the goal
Through my own goalpost
Reversing the norm
Of normality in the norm

If I should wear the dog collar
And call myself a Pastor
In pretence of shepherding
Heaven will take note
But never interfere
Like he never touched the dial
To reverse Calvary

If I should take the stethoscope
And hang it round my neck
And call myself a doctor
The world will dig the grit
And know whether I am
When my scalpel breaths
Of peaceful pain and living death

If I should call myself an engineer
And begin to measure the world

The world would know what type I am
When I build with steel upon the sand
And are tested by fiercest storm
And are rated by the most novice
When they wake from sleep

My Husband the Businessman

One day in one day out
My husband the businessman
Moves like honeybee on flowers
Adding to his barrels of honey in the stores
Going out each time to fend for more

His children don't really know him
They are sleeping when he jets out at dawn
They are sleeping when he jets in at dusk
On the sheet of no returns
Except the name of a money house at the top

This drive for very raw gold
Gave birth to the slave trade
Which in the hearts of traders never ever ended
Whenever one sees those mighty trade houses
Built on the backs of slaves

Again the drive for raw gold
Gave birth to those kingdom building parasites
That flew with wings of deity over nations
With the painkiller effect of new gold in the offing
From nations whose unholy grounds might never take their heads

What of the case of new commerce
Given to the late prophet's wife
A new-born star in oil trade
Together with her grown children
Who stood on the verge of becoming slaves

Not so the case of Ananias and Sapphira
Who neither traded in fruits nor precious stones
But traded their souls with the Devil for a lie

Hoping to become millionaires overnight
From a little title deed in their name

Where is my Free-Gold?

Where is the freehold gift God donated?
Could it be in your garment—isolated?

Why does my portion of land hang on a thread
In the speech potion from your puffed-up head?

Could it be that my own propaganda,
Is on the tail of your Party's *okada*?

My brother, on your heart stands a pine tree
That blossoms and gives birth to a spending spree.

A tree that feeds on the pains of others,
Must brew a bribe to be voted a star.

It even bribes the law to lose its sting—
Converting it from bee to sibling.

I imagine you sanitizing your hands
But not thinking of that for your brainpan.

Africa will rise when it dies to graft.
You too will rise when you defy the craft.

Oh Africa, the sting of smoke in my eyes,
When will your child aid and abet you to rise?

Africa, they say, the time is drawing near
When the earth shall be filled with the glory.

Africa, the continents will be present,
But you, will you still be playing with rent?

The continents will be in the glory
But you Africa, when? When Africa…?

Dinah
(based on Genesis 34)

The picnic at the gate is happening under dark clouds
And it follows on the heels of the picnic away from the gate
And there is talk of a piece of flesh
    A piece of flesh many pieces of flesh
    Can this be the pound of flesh
    Who will be the Daniel here
Can a piece of flesh really end the night of sorrow

Your brothers have opened a new door for you Dinah
A new direction that will only cut a path into the night
There are neither crickets seen nor any fireflies
    But there are watchmen of course
    And there are butchers of course
    But with no torchlight in your hands
What will ever end the night of sorrow

You almost fell when you were un-nailed from the wall
You seem so weak but please don't fall
You seem blinded by a river of tears but please don't fall
    A lot of blood still dripping
        With an owl waiting in the tree planted in your head
        And there is barter trade over your head
But strong muscles will now name for whom the bell tolls

A dirty young man will also choose his new direction
Whether to fly to heaven or to tread towards hell
He has so much hope with no river of tears
    But a river of remembrance
    He has collected what he wanted
    And has a bargain to give
Little does he know it is judgment day for him and others

Science without Humanity

"What sorrow awaits those who argue with their Creator? Does a clay pot argue with its maker? Does the clay dispute with the one who shapes it, saying, 'Stop, you're doing it wrong!' Does the pot exclaim, 'How clumsy can you be?' How terrible it would be if a newborn baby said to its father, 'Why was I born? or if it said to its mother, 'Why did you make me this way?' This is what the LORD says - the Holy One of Israel and your Creator: Do you question what I do for my children? Do you give me orders about the work of my hands?" Isaiah 45: 9 - 11 (NLT)

What did he bring?

What did he bring what did he bring
That handsome man from Ohio
Went up the moon and took the dust
And some artifacts costing
One hundred and eighty five million

What did he plant on that full moon
The little man went up the moon
And planted his footprints in moon dust
You may not see them but it cost
One hundred and eighty five million

How did they provoke that full moon
They planted one hundred mirrors
That will gossip about the moon
And its gravity and it cost
One hundred and eighty five million

What did America say
Nothing but offered him a wife
Baptized by the name alcohol
And he drank the dust costing them
One hundred and eighty five million

They sent a cancer hospital
And sent a university
And several acres of farming
When they sent those men costing
One hundred and eighty five million

DNA

Introduction level one:
>Red hair black hair brown hair
>Black eyes blue eyes green eyes
>Hawk nose Nubian nose African nose

Introduction level two:
>Sickle cell cancer cell brain cell
>Madness cell coughing cell Blindness cell
>Hyperactive cell slowness cell high speed cell

Introduction level three:
>Thieving culture adultery culture spying culture
>Fair complexion dark complexion Caucasian complexion
>Genius blood stupidity blood average blood

Responses level one:
>You have the same hair
>You have the same eyes
>You have the same nose

Responses level two:
>Great traces of sickle or cancer cell
>Great traces of madness or blindness
>And so you are flighty or nerveless

Responses level three:
>You can jump over the fence and break
>And now we see why you are albino
>And now we know why you are stupid

My DNA

Above my breath is my Grandfather's speed
Imaging a squirrel's fur in high weeds

Beneath my breath my grandma's drum for girls
Imaging tadpoles in a deep sea twirl

On the side are my father's soldier boots
Imaging the jigger toes of a stooge

On the back of my breath my uncle's greed
Imaging the goat's grabbing sense for grass

Inside my breath sparks of great Plato's thrills
Fly out of my great grand teacher's nostrils

Around my breath my grand aunt's lumpy breast
Hit me uppermost inside my hind rest

Half turning right on the clock of my breath
The torrents in my brother hit my head

Half turning left the liver of the chimp
Gave me the gimp in Noah's water limp

The Cambridge place said it all
The Cambridge place stamped my blood
And stamped my face
With a new kind of history
Now therefore let me rest my phase
So I rest my case…

Miss Queen Bee

Queen Bee, did I hear you well
On the quest for dis-integration
Or dis-family?
Sometimes my eardrums have not served me well.
Maybe you said integration
Or family.

If other anthills are anathema
To your existence,
What about your family far and near
In the Common-Wealth
Or un-Common-weds?
Will you bite them like pigs their piglets?

Do you remember the words of those anthems,
Those coronation anthems,
Oh Miss Queen Bee?
You must play them again
Before re-mounting your crown,
Where the gold thereof was purified by sweat and blood.

Oh that your soldier bees
Or worker bees
Might trot the globe again,
And un-march the good grounds turned sour
Matching them with bad grounds turned sweet
In the commonwealth.

The Eyeless God

The eyeless God needs your eyes,
That use two lenses,
Or more:
That he might see ...
Will you let him?

The earless God needs your ears,
That use two eardrums,
Or more:
That he might hear ...
Will you let him?

The nose-less God needs your nose,
That use two holes,
Or more?
That he might smell ...
Will you let him?

The mouthless God needs your mouth,
That uses two lips,
Or more:
That he might speak ...
Will you let him?

The armless God needs your arms,
That use two hands,
Or more:
That he might touch ...
Will you let him?

The legless God needs your legs,
That use two feet,
Or more:
That he might move ...
Will you let him?

The all-mind God needs your mind,
That uses two heads
Or more;
That he might think…
Will you let him?

The all-heart God needs your heart,
That uses two pipes
Or more;
That he might feel…
Will you let him?

Whatever you have,
God first had.
Whatever you give,
God first gave.
So just let him.

Message from Onan
(Genesis 38)

I thought we could agree
But since you can't agree
I have the power to throw you out
You better find another home

Imagine my new name with subtractions
Imagine my old name with additions
When you have no name whatsoever
You better find another home

There will be bloodshed with no tears
My blood will be shed after
But my democratic decision stands
You better find another home

I have no room for you in my inn
It is so unfortunate that I tickled your spirit
There is no manger and no cattle for you
You better find another home

You gave me a story of pain
Although you have no story
I will sell my story but not yours
You better find another home

Fare you well my friend
As an afterthought after no thought
You will not know my smiles
You better find another home

For me and the world you never were
And the democratic world never saw you
You violated my body with bad intentions
You better find another home

Poet in Residence

Under the mango tree
I am the Poet in Residence
Inspired by solitude
I took my harvest from the ground
Or call it the harvest by a bat
She had missed biting it
So I cleansed it before taking my bite
The envied mite envied from above

The only conversation between us
Was the biting of mangoes
I bit mine while she bit hers
Biting happening below
In response to biting happening above
In the epiphany born of solitude
In this residence of more than one writer
More than one poet I should say

The image from her writing
Is in full-fledged flight
Yet that of mine a full-fledged walk
In the spirit of walking about
And locating shade—mango shade
Poetry written indeed by teeth
In white ink—yes white ink
Used by writers before us

Around this moment are royal moments
From two worlds of empires
She writes in long-winded moments
I may never comprehend
And she cares little about the style from my empire
But she will care if I am to roast her
But no I will not roast her in that misreading
But lay her on a laboratory table soon

Religion without Sacrifice

"How much more shall the blood of Christ, who through the eternal Spirit offered himself without spot to God, purge your conscience from dead works to serve the living God?" Hebrews 9:14 (KJV)

The Slave Bible

Received Scripture, yes!
From the hands of slave masters, yes!
So what do you expect?
A well-doctored piece of literature,
Giving hope to its creator,
As hopeless as he is.

Well jacketed, yes!
Readable in English, yes!
So what do you expect?
The register of an English king,
With verses for his peace,
As hopeless as he is.

Well preserved, yes!
On an expensive shelf, yes!
So what do you expect?
Indexed by the best librarian,
For peace to flow through his mind,
As hopeless as he is.

Designed for slaves, yes!
Encouraging to masters, yes!
So what do you expect?
A sermon in the valley,
That will appease the master,
As hopeless as he is.

Written by the literate, yes!
Written for illiterates, yes!
So what do you expect?
A sermon for the poor,
With digestion direct by a master
As hopeless as he is.

Endorsed by the cream of society, yes!
Rejected by the cream of society, yes!
So what do you expect?
Justice cracked on all sides,
Dirtying the cream at the top,
As hopeless as they are.

Sacrificed With Tears

Great selfishness at work
Tearing the other into pieces
Like a piece of toilet tissue
For the toilet of my gut

Blood is dug out of the other's system
By piercing with a foreign body
A foreign body for pouring
The same into the toilet of my gut

I am battling with facts
To understand holiness
Away from strict unholiness
To feed the toilet of my gut

The first time I lay my hand
On the body of the other
That searched my eyes with her eyes
My blood ran cold into the toilet of my gut

I did the same with another animal
There was no difference with this other
Who looked at me in my eyes
And looked at the knife for the toilet of my gut

Is this anywhere near the toilet of my gut
Is there a sickness more diseased than the toilet of my gut
Insane and outdated clearly
For piercing the toilet of my gut

god is posh

god is posh in the ghettos
where trash is flash
of posh or purse
for a life wary of lush

god is ape in the forest
where games of doubt
are plagued by meshy minds
tried from angles of fuss

god is dream at home
where security is segregation
of measurement and hope
in the subplots of bonds

god is posh with poshy minds
that would throw only leftovers
of development riddles
toward the poor from riddled reigns

god is sold by priests that peep
torn blinds for chances of gold
once sold as the earnest
of development index in heaven

god is posh as posh is lush
for minds of buoyant flavours of taste
only tasted by the favoured
through invitations to parties by the posh

god is dreamer and foolish
for making man MAN
man is dreamer and clever
for making GOD god

God Is Standing There

My eyes are dim so I can't see well
the things I should see I can't see at all
My ears are deaf so I can't hear well
the things I should hear I can't hear at all
The lightning keeps flashing for blinded eyes
and the thunder keeps clapping for deafened ears
God is standing there
    Watching
        Waiting
            But I just can't tell

Mama your eyes may see fog
making everything foggy
Your ears may hear jingles
stamping everything jingle
Did you see your daughter
walking naked in the streets
God is standing there
    Watching
        Waiting
            But you just can't tell

Papa you stand so fine
but you can't see well
You speak so well
but you can't hear the bells
Now your son in ignorance
has started chasing your girls
God is standing there
    Watching
        Waiting
            But you just can't tell

Sister you go to Church
with your skirt just a mini
You sit in front of Pastor
not for seeing not for hearing
but to show your hidden beauty
to make him miss his steps
God is standing there
      Watching
           Waiting
                  But you just can't tell

Brother you stand for Satan in your office
with your long tailcoat
You sit for God in the Church
with your three-piece suit
But who are you talking to
and who are you feeling for
God is standing there
      Watching
           Waiting
                  But you just can't tell

You too are now a pastor
Shouting loud for communion
And God is there sharing
His body in the bread
And his blood in the wine
Make sure you don't stumble
God is standing there
      Watching
           Waiting
                  But you just can't tell

Pastor you went to a carnival
Preying on the girls like a carnivore
They went for each other saving your head
They stood at daggers drawn
While you remained unarmed
I don't know who you picked
God was standing there
        Watching
                Waiting
                        So you just couldn't tell

The sun has said goodnight
The moon is saying good morning
Is your dog collar same as in the day
How holy is holy in your times
How unholy is unholy in your times
When you crawl on the ground like one of your sheep
God is standing there
        Watching
                  Waiting
                        So you just can't tell

The Missing Shepherd
(For Bishop Albert Strieby Beah—1956 to 2017)

The Old Country Church
Stood for long in the valley
With forest and sheep and shepherds around
With their wives in a choir
Echoing anthems from above
And the pastor preached in a still small voice
But today of all days he is preaching to us all
Like he never did before

In that same Old Country Church
That stood in the valley for a looooong time
The shepherds came leaving sheep
And parting forest waters
Having heard the choir of angelic voices
And said we saw the bears of this valley… bears
But now we must see you as well
So he listened like he never did before

In the Old Country Church of the valley
Where the pastor listened to his flock
Who passed through forest fires
Minding blisters on the way
The pastor sat in his bishopric chair
Touching them one after the other
But today of all days is a new day
As he touched their hearts like he never touched before

They came from East
They came from West
They came from North
And they came from South
Mending new blisters from honey bees
Yet he queried them in a strange voice
Simon Peter do you love me
And he queried all like he never queried before

In that same Old Country Church
The flock came together
To listen to their pastor
And to be touched by their pastor
Because he had said a little while you shall see me
And a little while you shall not see me
He looked at them and only waved
He waved like he never waved before

From that Old Country Church
He took steps onward they knew not where
And opened his arms as if t'embrace
And said Woman behold thy son
And again said son behold thy Mother
And everywhere was silent
Because there was no noise in that grave
So he said I will rise again and you too will rise again

Sure enough those could not be the last
Words of a shepherd in limbo
Shepherd who shepherded sheep of colour
Shepherd whose guts were hated
Not like lions hating deer and their families
But kill for kill sakes in the jungle of doubts
So they wouldn't see him anymore
But for me the Lord is my Shepherd.

Join a Queue
(For Rev Violet O F T Kainwo when Received as a Minister on 13th August 1995)

You can see the stars ministers mini mini mini
Gliding high above the clouds and clouds and clouds
It is the way of servants who excel in the Spirit
Where base things do not stain their glows and glows and glows

Not only that they also wash the jigger toes of feet and feet and feet
Which they came to see where they wash feet and feet and feet
Look at those feet in motor tyres claiming their ground on motor roads
Towards the place where the displaced are more unplaced

I can see my sister and brother in their true servant colours
Aglow aglow aglow for those in the dark to see
Indeed the Master says the needy must see them
Before they go to Connaught or UNICEF or State House

The paraprofessionals know their cue and queue up in queues and queues
Of stars that call the children to play hand and foot games of games
Indeed they are here beckoning the new star to queue up
Come on sister you must catch the vogue and join a queue

The Table of Sacrifice

Did I ever kill in the name of Jesus
Did they go to heaven or hell
And did I go to heaven or hell
On visitation or permanent stay
Tell me did I or did I not

Were blacks ever laid on that table
Were other races there after them
Even they so full of ego-eggs did not know
They did not know even at point of slaughter
Tell me did they or did they not

Were Jews ever laid there as well
From Pharaoh to Herod to today
Did they cook their brains for supper
Did they know they would be alive today
Tell me did they or did they not

Were diamonds shaped for the slaughter
Or cobalt or bauxite or rutile
Were they sharpened by a tool of deceit
Be they holy books or unholy ticks
Tell me were they or were they not

Were selfish boundaries drawn in the process
To outscore the boundaries God had drawn
Did they fight at the table
Did they inadvertently cut their fingers
Tell me did they or did they not

My Funeral
(Based on Ecclesiastes 1:2)

Vanity of vanities, says the Preacher, all is vanity.
Will there be a funeral for me?
Maybe I will drown in the mouth of a shark,
Like my forebears on the high seas.
Or in a motor accident, seen but badly damaged,
At best a great case study for vultures.

Vanity of vanities, says the Preacher, all is vanity.
Who cares for the golden casket?
The casket, the procession or parade,
Will be for flashy eyes
Who never watched the sun at noon day.
But whoever cares for that shiny stuff?

Vanity of vanities, says the Preacher, all is vanity.
The bell might toll as for all humanity
So you should never send to ask
For whom the bell tolls,
Because it will only toll for humankind;
But whoever cares about that shaky question?

Vanity of vanities, says the Preacher, all is vanity.
Martin Luther King, Jr. said it all—
Please say at my funeral,
That Moses tried to be a Christian,
That Moses tried to love somebody,
And that Moses will answer to his Maker.

Vanity of vanities, says the Preacher, all is vanity.
Some will go for fanfare,
And an all-night vigil not ever attended in prayer,
And bore the ears of people with tributes;
But what is that to me when I'm gone?
My Maker knows my excesses, etcetera.

Holy Interventions

The voice that goes through fire
And says take off your shoes
Is power—unlimited power
So take them off

The voice that hits a palace
And says let my people go
Is power—unquestionable power
So let them go

The voice that hits the believer
And says go and make disciples
Is authority—unmistakable authority
So get up and go

The voice that looks at a mother-in-law
And says I must come with you
Is love—unmatchable love
So make them come

The voice that assesses man
And says chew the Book of the Law
Is life—immeasurable life
So chew it at once

The voice that calls my name
And says come out of the grave
Is Lord—the risen Lord
So I must come out

Politics without Principle

"When the godly are in authority, the people rejoice. But when the wicked are in power, they groan." Proverbs 29:2 (NLT)

a strong strong dance
(based on Matthew 11:17)

1. each coronation song

   hailed another moses
   yet none was christened so

   each tune then ended
   before the dance began
   the coming waves responded
   with their many many tunes
   and hence
         a strong strong dance
         which no one else could do

   let us catch the dancer's feet
   with a new new tune
   from the busy crowd
   and call him by his name

       or sing not

2. each toastmaster took the crown

to echo another clown

courting frowns after the rounds

each crown developed spikes

on the inside and on the outside

and the ruler lay straight

like snake among the people

and so

> a pastime on the canoe
>
> which only one could paddle

let us count each leader's words

like seeds from a water melon

so visible yet not so dark

planted on a hillside

> or list not

3. the space of elasticity

   has been time for harvesting

   yet none was named a farmer

   the harvest has been for one

   not even for the *fambul*

   the banks abroad grew bigger

as those at home grew smaller

and then

      the farce of an economy

      in a world of sombre economies

let us nurse this leader's words

on this very fertile ground

of land reclaimed from sea

and give them back their words

      or farm not

How are the Mighty Fallen?
(2 Samuel 1: 19 – 27)

All your glories, O Africa, are perishing on your heights.
O, how did this happen?

Publish it not in the streets of your exploiters,
those whose love can only enslave you,
before their daughters compose denigrating songs around your names.

O mountains of vain elitism,
may the bloody jewels you wear,
become hangmen's ropes around your necks;
and actually behead you.
for it is with those heads that you dream of beheading others

So many great slaves of the soil
have not returned from the dirty fields,
but fell by their own friendly blows.

Must I name your loyal slaves?
In life and in death they were African matter.
Indeed the names they gave
sprouted from their country blood.

O daughter of Africa,
weep for your heroes,
those that fed you with proverbs around the harvest fire,
and the forest swung to your tunes of love.

But how did we lose those mighty stuff?
No, they sleep on your heights, they are not lost!

Your eulogies are published in my blood.
For if I ever knew love,
you were my first teacher,
my conscientiser.

How indeed the mighty have fallen!
I wish you had become a pacifist,
for the weapons from carnal hands know no bounds!

A Letter to the Auditor General
(based on 2 Kings 12:15)

My Friend,
What would you call it?
I mean the misplacement of funds.
Borrowing with intent to swell up?
That sounds peacefully accommodating.
Embezzlement?
That is a heavy word from the sound of it.
Breach of trust?
That is a lighter expression for cowboys.
Misdemeanor?
This word reminds me of teachers, school boys and truancy.
Misappropriation?
Probably a husband might speak it into the ears of a careless wife.
Diversion?
More like a road construction style.
What would you call it?
Tell me, only tell me!

I Want A Wall

I want a wall to spite the hungry
Like I swore when I told the hungry
I want a wall with spikes on top
To burst the stomachs of the hungry
I want a wall

I want a wall to stop the insane
Like I told the civilised
A wall will bulldoze all latrines
Far far away from my wall
I want a wall

I want a wall a border wall
Where God can write a letter to me
And endorse my own creation
Of a garden of pure white roses
O want a wall

I want a wall billions of dollars long
So as to keep more dollars here
And mere desperate latrine mongers
Will not roll my dollars in place of toilet rolls
O want a wall

I want a wall where trumpeters can squat all day
And trump the excesses of humanity into oblivion
Watched from the corner of my eyes
In broad daylight
I want a wall

The Writing on the Wall

God is writing a letter in gold
A graduate from the best school
Where letter writing is by graduates
Of letter writers on walls

It is not toilet wall journalism
It is not bus station wall journalism
It is not street wall journalism
The journalist will write for all to see

A hand is moving on my wall
The writing is bold and clear
With no head for speeches
But a moving hand with speeches

The hand says it should not be
My son after me
Or my wife after me
The hand will not stop writing

The hand says we must measure the years
Anyone should sit in that chair
And pin it to the chair in gold
And posterity will measure the years

The Medes and the Persians are here
We should measure the years now
The navigators are here
We should measure the years now

Let the wall speak to those who can read
Let the wall articulate the mind of its author
For other poets to interpret
Like Falui in the morning sun

The Princess of My Heart
(For Diana, Princess of Wales 1961 -1997 based on Ecclesiastes 5:8)

The Princess of my heart indeed
Lived in the heart of death
She cut a canal for fresh tears
And hid the eyes of sunlight
That hit my blind at dawn

This path of printed pages raw
How royalty trod it for gain
But my lone star did spot the sign
Of printed minds as well
Who have to paint the paint

The phenomenal race course
Has bitter gold to give
No cheering stadia fans
To a game of non-starters
Where God himself is Ref

The Princess of the New Empire
Did you say they killed her
Who did what and where
The underdogs bear me out
Her life is red ink there

This full moon day has filled my eyes
With water of salt so deep
My Queen will ride into tomorrow
Her Saviour calls her home
Where angels praise and pray

The bridge that tripped her soul from sole
Hunted her for every catch

Consuming her love in anger bent
Herself a swinging bridge
Upon pent-up pen pals

Let Me Be Wrong

That you brought your sister down
First with words then with a bullet
In order to catch the pinnacle of power
For just a few years ahead
Yet stand to lose her for the rest of life
Let me be wrong in believing
That I share this space with you

That you fed someone's youth with falsehood
And made them commit this against humanity
For a post that is not permanently posted
Like the sleep and wake of time
In the name of policies undefined
Let me be wrong in believing
That I share this space with you

That you pumped fuel into election results
And lighted it with a spark of bad words
Leading to a horror movie
On the arena where dogs eat dogs
In the pathway to State House
Let me be wrong in believing
That I share this space with you

That you could promise the moon
When not behind Armstrong's lenses
When not carrying the gift of moon dust
When not wearing the mask for moon dust
But you wear a mask to hide your identity
Let me be wrong in believing
That I share this space with you

That you could hit Ikemefuna
Repeatedly towards his death
Is a gross show of cowardice
But since you sold your eyes of shame
I am never surprised by any behavior of yours
Let me be wrong in believing
That I share this space with you

www.ingramcontent.com/pod-product-compliance
Lightning Source LLC
Chambersburg PA
CBHW052115110526
44592CB00013B/1624